They Shall Be HEARD

Susan B. Anthony & Elizabeth Cady Stanton

21

They Shall Be HEARD
Susan B. Anthony & Elizabeth Cady Stanton

By Kate Connell

Alex Haley, General Editor

Illustrations by Barbara Kiwak

STECK-VAUGHN
C O M P A N Y

A Subsidiary of National Education Corporation

Published by Steck-Vaughn Company.

Text, illustrations, and cover art © 1993 by Dialogue Systems, Inc., 627 Broadway, New York, New York 10012.

Cover art by Barbara Kiwak

Printed in the United States of America
1 2 3 4 5 6 7 8 9 R 98 97 96 95 94 93 92

Library of Congress Cataloging-in-Publication Data

Connell, Kate, 1954–
    They shall be heard: the story of Susan B. Anthony and
Elizabeth Cady Stanton / Kate Connell; illustrator, Barbara
Kiwak.
        p. cm.—(Stories of America)
    Summary: Describes the work of Susan B. Anthony and
Elizabeth Cady Stanton for the women's suffrage movement.
    ISBN 0-8114-7228-0.—ISBN 0-8114-8068-2 (softcover)
    1. Feminists—United States—Biography—Juvenile literature.
2. Suffragettes—United States—Biography—Juvenile literature.
3. Anthony, Susan B. (Susan Brownell), 1820–1906—Juvenile lit-
erature. [1. Anthony, Susan B. (Susan Brownell). 2. Stanton,
Elizabeth Cady, 1815–1902. 3. Feminists. 4. Women's rights.]
I. Kiwak, Barbara, ill. II. Title. III. Series.
HQ1412.C65 1993
324.6'23'092—dc20
[B]   92–18088
                                                              CIP
                                                               AC

ISBN 0-8114-7228-0 (Hardcover)
ISBN 0-8114-8068-2 (Softcover)

Introduction
by Alex Haley, General Editor

The tools of freedom are simple ones. They are the right to vote, the right to speak freely, and the right to a trial by a jury of one's peers. There are others, but these three are the hammers, saws, and nails of freedom's tool kit. You cannot build a just society unless all citizens have access to these tools.

The United States of America was almost 150 years old before women—half its population at any given time—were given the right to vote. It took even longer before women were allowed to serve on juries, which means that when a woman was tried in a court of law, she was judged only by men. Speech, too, was limited—fathers, husbands, or brothers could forbid a woman from voicing her opinion on a matter of concern to her.

The story you are about to read tells how women began the job of acquiring the tools of freedom. It is a story of determination, courage, and persistence.

We would like to thank the librarians at the Arthur and Elizabeth Schlesinger Library on the History of Women in America at Radcliffe College for their help.

Contents

Prologue

It didn't seem like the kind of day that would bring bad news, but it was.

The sun sparkled and the air was crisp. The sky was a deep, endless blue. Great gusts of wind brought red and gold leaves swirling to the ground from the big old trees that stood about the house. It was a perfect October day in 1902— not a gloomy sort of day at all.

From the window of her upstairs study, Susan B. Anthony could see the autumn leaves fly by. She sat in her usual chair, surrounded by stacks of papers and piles of books. Her hair was white, her features sharp and wrinkled. Eighty-two she was, and more and more lately, she felt her age.

A quiet knock sounded at the door and Ida Harper entered. She was a writer who was living with Susan while she wrote Susan's biography. Ida had a telegram in her hand and a worried look on her face. Reluctantly she handed the telegram to Susan, who opened it with a shaky hand.

It was from her best friend's daughter. It said: "Mother passed away today."

The shadows in the room seemed to deepen all at once. Susan let the telegram fall into her lap. She turned to the portrait hanging on the wall and looked hard at the face of her friend of fifty years. It was almost as though she were willing Elizabeth Cady Stanton back to life, willing her to talk to her one more time. The painting didn't speak, but Susan's gaze never wavered. Ida stole away, leaving Susan to her grief and her memories.

PART ONE

1

The Meeting

Had it really been 51 years since she had met Elizabeth Cady Stanton for the first time? Since she had stood on the street corner in Seneca Falls, nervously smoothing her grey gloves, waiting to be introduced?

Looking back on it now, it seemed like the most fateful moment of Susan's life. It was as if Fate had personally reached down and placed her on that corner just when Mrs. Stanton was passing by. As if they were meant to become best friends and go on to lead the women's rights movement.

But it didn't seem that way at the time. They met sometime in the spring of 1851—the exact date had escaped Susan long ago. She had gone to Seneca Falls for an anti-slavery meeting, she remembered. Amelia Bloomer had invited her. Little Mrs. Bloomer, the one who made the short dress so popular it came to be called "bloomers." She published the pattern for bloomers in her monthly paper. And she wore them longer than anyone. Eight years, wasn't it?

What a trial that dress was! Who would think that a dress that came to below the knee, with pantaloons worn underneath, would cause such a fuss? But it did. It was impossible to wear it on the street without a group of dirty-faced boys tagging after you hollering "breeches!" Even Mrs. Bloomer had to stop wearing it. A very sensible fashion, bloomers, but just not worth the trouble.

But Susan's mind was wandering. Where was she? Oh yes, she and Mrs. Bloomer had gone to an anti-slavery meeting. First the British abolitionist George Thompson spoke. Then the great William Lloyd Garrison got up and electrified everyone the way he always did. It fairly stirred her soul to hear him.

But the best came later. On the way home, Mrs. Bloomer spotted Mrs. Stanton walking with those two gentlemen, and offered to introduce

Susan to her. Susan hardly knew what to think as she shook Mrs. Stanton's hand. Could this be the woman who had demanded the right to vote—on a public platform!—three years before? The woman the newspapers had called dangerous and unnatural? She seemed so . . . normal.

Mrs. Stanton was short, shorter than Susan by several inches. She was very plump and very pretty, with dark hair done up in curls. Her frank blue eyes seemed to bore right into Susan's. She appeared to take one look at Susan—at her smooth hair drawn back into a bun, her neat grey dress, her matching grey hat with the blue ribbons, her warm smile—and to like what she saw.

Susan couldn't remember now what they talked about—the meeting, most likely. It couldn't have been very important, but something "clicked." They liked each other immediately. Alas, they had exchanged no more than a few words before Mrs. Stanton had to fly. She simply couldn't linger, what with a dinner to see to, and three mischievous boys and a baby at home. She shook Susan's hand warmly and promised to write—and then she was gone.

Susan went home to Rochester after that and a letter soon arrived from Mrs. Stanton, inviting

Susan to visit. Susan answered with pleasure, the visit was arranged, and a lively correspondence began. Susan quite properly addressed her new friend, who was five years her elder and famous, as "Mrs. Stanton." With her usual self-assurance, Mrs. Stanton began her letters with a familiar "Dear Susan." And though they came to be the best of friends, to each other they remained Susan and Mrs. Stanton for the next half century.

2

The Everlasting No

Susan might well have been surprised at how much Mrs. Stanton seemed to be just like other women. For any woman who could get up in front of a crowd of people and demand the right to vote, unheard of in those days, couldn't be just like other women. Not possibly. And yet Mrs. Stanton was a loyal wife and a devoted mother, an excellent housekeeper and a charming hostess. All of the things a nineteenth-century woman was supposed to be, Mrs. Stanton was.

Or was she? That was the puzzle.

The pieces of that puzzle were buried in the past. Elizabeth Cady Stanton was born in 1815, the middle daughter of a well-to-do family from

Johnstown, New York. Her father, Daniel Cady, was a respected judge and landowner. Her mother, a tall, elegant woman, was Margaret Livingston Cady, one of *the* Livingstons. The Livingstons were among the oldest and wealthiest families in the state.

Elizabeth's family wasn't exactly rich, but they were very far from poor. Their big house was the finest in Johnstown. Its cellar and attic bulged with barrels of nuts and apples, vegetables and salted meats, cider and butter, cakes of maple sugar and bunches of dried herbs. There was money enough for servants, horses and carriages, new dresses every year, and modest presents at Christmastime. No, Elizabeth Cady never lacked the things money could buy.

The Cady household was a strict one, though. Looking back on her childhood, Mrs. Stanton wrote that "fear, rather than love, of God and parents alike, predominated."[1] A Scottish nanny with a sharp tongue and an even sharper eye was employed to keep the Cady children in line. There was a whole host of things they weren't allowed to do: play in the attic, wade in the nearby creek,

---

[1] ruled

climb the snow-covered woodpile in winter. If it was noisy, or dirty, or fun, it was usually against the rules.

No wonder, then, that Elizabeth Cady developed a rebellious streak a mile wide. "I am so tired of that everlasting no! no! no!" she complained to her nurse one day as she sat looking out the nursery window. "At school, at home, everywhere it is *no*! Even at church all the commandments begin 'Thou shalt not.' I suppose God will say 'no' to all we like in the next world, just as you do here."

The nurse was shocked and gave Elizabeth a good round scolding for her impudence. Meanwhile her sister Margaret, playing in the corner, was all ears.

"I tell you what to do," Margaret whispered when the nurse had left the room. "Hereafter let us act as we choose, without asking."

"Then we shall be punished," Elizabeth countered.

"Suppose we are," said Margaret, "we shall have had our fun at any rate, and that is better than to mind the everlasting 'no' and not have any fun at all."

Elizabeth had to admit that Margaret had a

point. The sisters decided to adopt this new philosophy, come what may. After that, whenever Elizabeth hesitated, Margaret would give her a tug and say "Oh come along!" At times they got into a good bit of trouble, but they learned not to mind it.

When Elizabeth was eleven, tragedy struck the Cady family. Elizabeth's older brother, Eleazar, died. He had just graduated from college. This would have been a terrible loss for any family, but for the Cadys—at least for Judge Cady—it was especially hard. Hard because, of the six Cady children, five were girls. Eleazar was the only boy and he was gone.

Elizabeth's father never got over it. A son was all he had ever wanted. Only a son could become a lawyer and take over his business. Only a son could inherit his fortune. By law and by custom, girls couldn't do such things. Girls were expected to do one thing and one thing only when they grew up, and that was get married. Once a woman married, everything she owned became her husband's property.

Elizabeth knew that Eleazar was her father's

favorite, but she didn't mind. He was her favorite, too. Everyone loved him. When he died, the Cadys went into mourning. The house was draped in black. Everyone had to walk on tiptoe and speak in whispers, out of respect for the body of her dead brother lying in his coffin in the parlor.

In this unnatural quiet, Elizabeth heard a sob coming from the parlor. Stealing in, she found her father sitting by the coffin, lost in grief. She climbed on his lap and rested her head lovingly against his chest. What could she say? What could she do to comfort him? Elizabeth pondered this as they sat in silence. Finally her father heaved a great sigh.

"Oh my daughter," he said sadly, "I wish you were a boy."

Elizabeth raised her startled face to look at him, but he wasn't looking at her. She became thoughtful. Well, she decided to herself, if it will make Father happy, I'll *be* like a boy. She wrapped her arms around his neck and whispered, "I will try to be all my brother was."

And so Elizabeth Cady spent the rest of her girlhood trying to be a son to her father. She learned to ride and jump a horse, because that's what boys did. She pored over her father's law

books and hung around his office, debating with his law students. She went to an all-boys school and learned Greek, because that's what boys studied. At graduation, she won a prize for her Greek.

Succeeding at all these things gave Elizabeth the feeling that she could do anything if she put her mind to it. Her accomplishments gave her a self-confidence that never deserted her. But they didn't give her what she wanted the most: her father's approval. Instead of praising his daughter, Judge Cady only shook his head and said what a shame it was that she was a girl.

No matter what she did, no matter how hard she tried, Elizabeth couldn't please her father. Finally, when she was 23, she stopped trying. That was the year she fell in love with Henry Stanton.

She met Henry at her cousin's house. He was twelve years older than she, tall, handsome, charming, a good dancer—and an abolitionist. As an agent for the American Anti-Slavery Society, he got paid (not very much) to travel around and get people fired up about slavery by making radical speeches against it. That was his job, and he was very good at it.

Judge Cady was absolutely against the match. No daughter of *his* was going to marry a man who had no money to speak of and no profession other than stirring up trouble. He wouldn't stand for it!

But Elizabeth married Henry anyway in 1840. It was her first grown-up act of rebellion—the first of many, as it turned out.

The day after the wedding, Henry and Elizabeth set sail for London, England. Henry had abolitionist business there, so they decided to make a wedding trip out of it.

Henry's business was at the World Anti-Slavery Convention. This was an enormous gathering of abolitionists from all over the English-speaking world. Henry had been elected to represent the United States at the convention.

In those days, such conventions were quite commonplace. Reformers held them all the time, to air their ideas and attract attention to their causes. They would meet every day for hours on end, hundreds and hundreds of people in one vast hall. Leading reformers would take turns making speeches and everyone else would listen. Sooner or later someone would disagree and interrupt and then a debate would begin. Some conventions were deadly dull. Others were nothing short of chaos.

In London, Henry and Elizabeth both went to the convention—he as a delegate, and she as a spectator. No sooner had it started than a noisy debate arose over whether or not six women delegates from America should be allowed to participate. Elizabeth, quite naturally, thought they should be. They'd been elected fair and square, just as Henry had.

But most of the men, especially the British men, did not agree. It just wasn't "proper," they argued, for women to mix in the public affairs of men. The debate went back and forth. At one point Henry Stanton rose and made a brief, clever speech. When he sat down, no one was sure just which side he had taken.

Finally the question was put to a vote. The verdict: the women delegates would not be admitted. They must sit in a screened-off area reserved for women and observers.

How infuriating! The everlasting no all over again! At that moment, a spark of anger in Elizabeth burst into flame. These men were exactly like her father. It didn't matter to them how well you could do something. It only mattered what sex you were. And for some stupid reason which she had yet to figure out, if you were female you just didn't count.

The anger never left Elizabeth after that. On her last day in London, it gave her an idea. She'd spent the day walking the streets arm in arm with Lucretia Mott. Mrs. Mott was one of the women who had been shut out of the convention. In quiet voices they had talked the whole thing over. That's when it came to her: why couldn't they hold their *own* convention, to discuss the many wrongs against women—and the rights women needed to fix them?

The Seneca Falls Convention

On July 14, 1848, an announcement appeared in the *Seneca County Courier.* A convention "to discuss the social, civil, and religious condition and rights of women" was to be held the next week at the Methodist Church. Women, it said, were "earnestly invited to attend."

Five days later, the roads into Seneca Falls were clogged with carriages. The church was a sea of bonnets, with quite a number of bare male heads among them. People had come from miles around, and the church was filled to bursting.

On a raised wooden platform at the front of the church sat a very nervous Elizabeth Cady Stanton. Eight years had passed since she and

Mrs. Mott had first talked about doing this. Eight busy years filled with children and housekeeping. But at last it was happening. She and Mrs. Mott were finally holding that convention.

Talking about it had been one thing. Even putting the announcement in the paper had been easy. But now she, Elizabeth Cady Stanton, actually had to stand up in front of all those people—men, too—and talk! She had never felt so shy in all her life.

Oh, it was all right for Mrs. Mott. She was a Quaker preacher and was used to speaking before an audience. But Elizabeth had never done such a thing. What woman (outside of a Quaker meeting) had? Public speaking was another one of those things that "nice" women didn't do. It was considered unfeminine, and in 1848, unfeminine was about the worst thing a woman could be. Well, at least Lucretia's husband would preside. None of the women, not even Mrs. Mott, felt equal to that.

Besides her own speech, Elizabeth had written a special statement for the occasion. She called it a "Declaration of Sentiments." It stated women's grievances—eighteen in all—and it demanded changes. In those days, nearly every-

one knew the Declaration of Independence by heart, so she used that as her model. "We hold these truths to be self-evident," she boldly declared, "that all men and women are created equal. . . ."

On the first day of the convention, the entire document was read aloud and several people, Mrs. Stanton included, got up and spoke. (She did well despite her stage fright.) On the second day it was read again and each paragraph was debated. Finally a vote was taken, the Declaration was adopted, and it was signed by 68 women and 32 men. All in all, Mrs. Stanton decided afterward, it was a huge success.

Then the newspapers came out with their reports, and the women wondered what on earth they had done. "Was there ever such a dreadful revolt?" asked the *Oneida Whig* in alarm. Lots of people were asking themselves the same question.

For Mrs. Stanton had done the unthinkable. She had put into the Declaration something so new, so revolutionary, that even Mrs. Mott objected to it.

"Resolved," Mrs. Stanton had written, "that it is the duty of the women of this country to secure themselves their sacred right to the elective franchise." In other words, she wanted the right to vote.

"But Lizzie," Mrs. Mott had said reproachfully, "thee will make us look ridiculous."

Mrs. Stanton didn't care. She hadn't studied her father's law books all those years for nothing. She knew that injustice toward women was not merely a custom—it was the law.

It was actually illegal for a married woman to keep any money she earned. Her earnings belonged to her husband.

It was illegal for her to buy or sell a house or a piece of land, to borrow money from a bank, or to own a business. Her husband had to do these things for her.

If for some reason she was divorced—which was a scandal in itself—the law gave her husband custody of the children. Mothers had no rights.

Knowing all this, Elizabeth Cady Stanton insisted on putting the right to vote into her Declaration. She didn't care what Mrs. Mott said. She didn't care that Henry was so embarrassed that he left town until the convention was over. How else were women ever going to change the laws except by electing lawmakers to do it, or by getting elected themselves? And they couldn't do that if they couldn't vote. It was plain common sense.

But a lot of people didn't think so. One newspaper called it a "most shocking and unnatural incident. . . . If our ladies will insist on voting and legislating,[2] where, gentlemen, will be our dinners and our elbows? Where our domestic firesides and the holes in our stockings?" Many papers resorted to ridicule, with headlines like "Hen Convention" and "The Reign of Petticoats." The *Philadelphia Public Ledger* stated flatly, "A woman is nobody."

There was one advantage to all the bad press, however. It gave the new cause a lot of publicity.

"It will start women thinking," Mrs. Stanton wrote excitedly to Mrs. Mott a few days later, "and men, too, and when men and women think about a new question, the first step in progress is taken. The great fault of mankind," she added in her decided way, "is that it will not think!"

---

[2] making laws

4

Susan

Mrs. Stanton was right. The Seneca Falls Convention did set people to thinking. Among them was Susan B. Anthony.

In 1848, the year of the convention, Susan Anthony was 28 years old. She was nobody famous, just a schoolteacher earning her own money and spending most of it on nice clothes. Actually, around the time that Mrs. Stanton was demanding the vote, Susan was enjoying a shopping spree. She bought a new silk bonnet with a pink lining and had two old dresses made over. There was a mantilla[3] she had her eye on, too,

---

[3] a short cape or cloak

that cost $30. She vowed not to buy it—it was really too extravagant—but she did anyway. "There is not a mantilla in town like mine," she wrote afterward.

Susan had been teaching for nearly ten years, but she hadn't always spent her money on clothes. For a long time she sent every spare penny home to her father and mother. The Anthonys had fallen on hard times. Most people in those days thought it was something of a disgrace for a woman to work outside the home. But Susan wasn't one of them. It never occurred to her to do anything but get a job and help out. That was the way she was raised.

Susan was born in 1820 in Adams, Massachusetts. She was one of seven children, two boys and five girls. Her father, Daniel Anthony, had built a small cotton mill there and made a good living. When Susan was six, her father decided to move to Battenville, New York, to start a cotton factory and a general store. The factory prospered, and before long Mr. Anthony had opened another one a few miles down river.

By the time Susan was twelve, the Anthonys had grown wealthy. Daniel Anthony started building a fine new house for his family—all brick, with fifteen rooms. But some things didn't change. Daniel Anthony was a Quaker, and at heart he was a plain man. Plain living would always be his way no matter how much money he had.

Take servants, for example. Unlike the Cadys, who had a nanny and a porter and a coachman and a cook, the Anthonys had no servants. Lucy Anthony, Susan's mother, did every stitch of housework herself with the help of her three oldest daughters, Guelma, Susan, and Hannah. Back in Adams, eleven of their mill hands had boarded in the house with them. That meant cooking breakfast, lunch, and dinner for sixteen people every day. They could spend a whole day just baking bread, twenty loaves at a time. Laundry was the worst chore, because the water had to be hauled to the house from a stream—hundreds of pounds of water for one wash. But Lucy and the girls did it.

In Battenville the factory workers lived in their own small houses, built for them by Daniel Anthony. But when the new house was begun, a dozen bricklayers were hired—and promptly moved in with the Anthonys. The cooking, sewing, and washing seemed endless. It made a twelve-hour day in the factory seem easy.

Maybe that was why when one of the factory women fell sick, Susan and Hannah jumped at the chance to substitute for her. They both begged for the job, but only one girl was needed. Finally their parents decided that the girls would flip a coin. Whoever won would split her wages—three dollars for two weeks—with the other sister. Susan won.

Despite the hard work, the Anthonys were happy. Love, not fear, ruled their household. Daniel Anthony was an unusual man for his time. He held deep convictions, and one of those convictions was that all human beings were equal in the sight of God. He taught his daughters to be as self-reliant as his sons. When Susan came home from school one day and reported that her teacher, a man, had refused to teach her long division because she was a girl, Daniel Anthony pulled his children out of school and started a home school.

Of course Daniel Anthony wasn't perfect. He believed that slavery was wrong. Yet he made his living milling cotton that had been grown and picked by southern slaves. When Susan was eleven, she asked her father to make one of the women overseer of the factory. He dismissed the idea. "It would never do to have a woman over-seer in the mill," he said, and that was the end of it. He didn't explain why it would never do. It just wouldn't.

Most of the time, though, he tried to live up to his beliefs. As a temperance man, for example, he wouldn't take even a sip of wine. He wouldn't allow alcohol in his house. And any of his workers who drank didn't work for him for long.

When he opened the Battenville store, he thought long and hard about whether or not to sell rum and whiskey. He decided not to. His mill partner warned him that he'd never stay in business that way, but Daniel Anthony stuck to his decision—and he stayed in business.

Mr. Anthony also refused to pay taxes. As a Quaker, he thought it was wrong to support a government that waged war. "I shall not voluntarily pay these taxes," he would say to the tax collector, laying his purse on the table. "If thee wants to rifle in my pocketbook, thee can do so."

With such a father to learn from, and such a family to love, Susan was a happy child. She even wrote a poem, at the age of 14, in praise of home and family. But her father could see that in one way, home was limiting his daughters. Guelma and Susan had started taking summer teaching jobs. They really needed more education than he could give them at home.

So Daniel Anthony quietly began sending away to Quaker boarding schools for brochures. One interested him particularly. It was from Deborah Moulson's Female Seminary near Philadelphia. It stated that ". . . the principles of Humility, Morality, and love of Virtue will receive particular attention." That, he decided, was the place for his daughters.

5

Miss Moulson's School

It was cold and overcast, as dreary as a day at the end of November can be. The murky waters of New York harbor seemed to absorb, rather than reflect, the early morning light. Both sky and water were a dull, unflinching grey.

Susan stood at the rail of the steamboat as it churned its way out of the harbor. She gazed without blinking into the foaming water. It fascinated her—the endlessly changing water with its curling, tossing, dancing foam. She watched, mesmerized, and thought about what was coming.

At the age of 17, Susan was leaving home for the first time in her life. Not forever—and not by herself—but for a long time, perhaps a year. Her

father was taking her to school near Philadelphia. Guelma was already there and that, at least, was a comfort. Susan wouldn't be completely alone.

But Susan was scared. She had never been away from home before. Sooner or later her father would have to leave her, and oh how hard that would be! And it was. That afternoon they reached Philadelphia, saw some sights, and went to the school. When her father left her at around nine that night, Susan couldn't even speak to say goodbye. She went to her room and wept. For days afterward the memory of her father's leaving made the tears rise up in her throat so that she had to struggle to hold them back.

✻

Six weeks later, in the beginning of January 1838, Susan sat in the window seat of her room at school. She had decided to start a diary. Dipping her quill pen carefully in ink, she began to write, very slowly and neatly, on foolscap paper. "A little history of events," she began, "taken occasionally from the time I left home. . . . "

Into her "little history" she poured all her trials at school, and there were many. To be sure, she recorded the weather, what time she rose each day, what she studied, and whether or not she got a letter from home. But more than once Susan turned to her diary in utter anguish. For the headmistress, Deborah Moulson, was an exceedingly strict woman, and Susan seemed always to be doing something wrong.

One afternoon in February, Deborah came into Susan's class and began examining the girls' writing books. The first girl whose book she looked at earned a severe scolding. Slowly she walked among the desks. She stopped at another, looked, and said nothing at all. Susan, thinking her writing had improved, offered her book for Deborah's inspection.

But Susan had thought wrong. Deborah took the book and, in front of the whole class, pointed out one flaw after another in Susan's penmanship, finally declaring that teaching such a student was a waste of time. Susan felt herself flush all over with humiliation. The blood pounded in her ears. When the class moved on to reading, she was called on to read and did so, without even knowing what she was doing.

"When school was out," she later wrote, "I first went to the privy[4] [to] give vent to my tears, and

---

[4] bathroom

then back to the house and upstairs where without restraint I indulged in tears. . . . feel as if I could not go in D's sight."

Poor earnest Susan! She had always had the most understanding of teachers—her own father. Deborah Moulson was nothing like him. To make things worse, Susan had trouble with her eyes which made it hard to read sometimes. "Often do their nonconformance[5] mortify this frail heart, when attempting to read in class," she wrote.

She tried awfully hard to be good. Her diary was filled with little prayers. "O to improve," she wrote. "O may I be more thoughtful . . . ." "O may this heart become more and more refined, until nothing shall remain but perfect purity." But scarcely a week passed without Susan being made to feel that she had committed some horrendous crime.

In February, Susan got bad news from her father. Business had been going downhill since before she started at the school, though he had managed to send her anyway. But a nationwide financial panic had pushed him over the edge. He was nearly bankrupt. He couldn't pay his debts, couldn't keep the factory or the house. She could

---

[5] One of Susan's eyes wandered.

finish out the term, since it was already paid for, but then she must come home.

May of 1838 found Susan back in Battenville, watching her beloved home disintegrate before her eyes. An auction was held to sell off their possessions, so that Daniel Anthony could pay some of his debts. Nothing was too small or too personal to be sold: Lucy Anthony's wedding presents, furniture, books, clothing, the girls' underclothes, her parents' spectacles, the boys' pocketknives. Everything went on the auction block, right down to the coffee and tea in the kitchen. Luckily for the family, Lucy Anthony's brother, Uncle Joshua Read, bought up their dearest possessions and gave them back.

The Anthonys moved to Hardscrabble, a nearby village of "brown hovels and broken rough appearance." They rented an old tavern and took in boarders to help make ends meet. Nothing now remained for Susan but to find a teaching job, which she quickly did. "I again left my home to mingle with strangers," she wrote, "which seems to be my lot."

6

Food for Thought

For the next ten years, summer and winter, Susan taught school. She moved from town to town until, in 1848, she found herself head-mistress of the female department at the Canajoharie Academy in upstate New York.

It was the end of her second year there, and Susan was beginning to tire of teaching. She wasn't sure why. She was good at it, without question. When Susan got up in front of a class-room, there wasn't a hint of the trembling school-girl she had once been at Deborah Moulson's. She was liked by everyone—her students, her neigh-bors, and the various suitors who hovered about. For the first time in her life she had money to spend on herself. Her taste in clothes was anything but plain; for a while her wardrobe became very un-Quakerlike.

But she wasn't satisfied. She began to wonder if teaching was what she really wanted to do for the rest of her life. She didn't want to get married. Guelma and Hannah both had, but Susan didn't envy them. She had never yet met a man she liked or respected enough to marry. Her independence was too important to be given up for just anyone.

Susan was restless. In one way she hadn't changed since her school days, and that was in her earnest desire to be good. "O to improve . . . ." She still felt that. She wanted to live an upright life. She wanted to change the world and make it better—but how? She didn't know.

Susan decided to visit her parents. She hadn't been home for a visit since she had first arrived in Canajoharie two years before. Her parents now lived on a farm near Rochester, New York. Her father was doing well at last in the insurance business.

So in August of 1848—a month after Mrs. Stanton, halfway across the state, had begun agitating for women's rights—Susan put on one of her newly made-over dresses and the silk bonnet with the pink lining and boarded the train for Rochester. When she got there, she had a surprise.

The household was buzzing with talk of a second women's rights convention held right there in Rochester. Her parents, her youngest sister Mary, and her cousin had all gone to it. Mrs. Elizabeth Cady Stanton had spoken and her Declaration of Sentiments had been passed around. The Anthonys had signed it. And cousin Abigail had actually presided over the meeting!

Of course Susan had read about the Seneca Falls Convention the month before. Who hadn't? It had aroused her curiosity—and tickled her funny bone. That's right; Susan was amused by Mrs. Stanton's audacity, but she couldn't take it seriously. She was astonished that her family had.

Not that Susan was against rights for women. She just wasn't convinced that they were very important. What Susan thought the country needed most was temperance and abolition. She had learned both at her father's knee. Those two reforms, she believed, could truly make the world a better place.

So she went back to Canajoharie and put in one more dreary year. Then in 1849, she quit her teaching job and moved home to manage the family farm. She joined the Daughters of Temperance. And she began attending anti-slavery meetings.

Over the next two years Susan went to every abolitionist meeting she could. She organized a new chapter of the Daughters of Temperance. She even made a speech—her first ever—at one of their meetings. She began to travel and her circle widened. She made a lot of new friends among the reformers. One of them was Amelia Bloomer, a temperance crusader from Seneca Falls who invited Susan to visit in March of 1851.

And that was how Susan finally got to meet the much-talked-about radical, the audacious woman herself, Elizabeth Cady Stanton. A woman whose background and education couldn't have been more different from Susan's. But who took an immediate liking to Susan—a liking that Susan returned with all her heart.

PART TWO

7

Mrs. Stanton's Struggles

It was late, and the Stanton house was almost completely dark. Upstairs, the boys had been asleep for hours. In the back of the house a single light gleamed. Amelia Willard, the Stantons' new housekeeper, was in the kitchen mixing bread for the next day.

Another light, dim and flickering, moved through the house like a ghost. It was Mrs. Stanton. Candle in hand, she entered the dining room. She fumbled a moment as she lit the lamp on the round mahogany table. She was so tired tonight. Perhaps this once she would just go up to bed. But that was wishful thinking and she knew it. Late in the evening was the only time Mrs.

Stanton ever had to herself. If she didn't write to Susan tonight the letter wouldn't reach her in time.

Mrs. Stanton eased herself into a chair and pulled ink and paper toward her. There was so much she wanted to say. First of all, the temperance question. "My Dear Friend," she began, "I think you are doing up the temperance business just right . . . ."

Just a few months ago, in January, Susan had gone to a meeting of the Sons of Temperance in Albany. She was admitted after showing that she was a member of the Rochester "Daughters." Taking her seat with the other women there, she sat silently while the men carried on the business of the meeting. Before long Susan grew restless and wanted to say something. She rose from her seat, only to have the president of the meeting tell her coldly to sit down, as "the sisters were not invited there to speak but to listen and learn."

Mrs. Stanton could well imagine the flush of humiliation and pure anger that rose up in her friend. Susan gave the man one black look, then turned on her heel and walked out. A few other women got up and followed her. Susan then called her own meeting, invited the newspapers, and announced that the women would form their own organization: the Women's State Temperance Society.

Mrs. Stanton was delighted at Susan's protest. It was about time temperance women asserted their rights! And Susan, a woman after her own heart, was just the woman to do it. When Susan called a convention to be held April 20 in Rochester, Mrs. Stanton readily agreed to help in whatever way she could.

But it was already April 2. Mrs. Stanton knew that she was expected to be at the convention. Susan was planning to nominate her for president of the society. But Mrs. Stanton was beginning to doubt whether she could go. There was so much to do, managing the house and looking after the children. Why, she hadn't spoken in public since the Rochester convention in 1848. That was three and a half years ago. Sometimes she wondered if she ever would again.

Things had been a *little* easier lately. She had Amelia now to share the baking, preserving, sewing, housekeeping, laundry, and children. And with her two oldest, Neil and Kit, away at boarding school this year, things were a bit less chaotic around the house. She did miss them, though.

Imagine Neil writing and asking her not to visit them "in costume"! Wearing the short dress, he meant.

"You do not wish me to visit you in a short dress!" she had written back. "Why, my dear child, I have no other. . . . You want me to be like other people. You do not like to have me laughed at. You must learn not to care for what foolish people say . . . no matter if ignorant silly persons do laugh."

Neil just didn't realize what a godsend the short dress was. Without it, she would be even less able to do all that had to be done around the house. Just walking up the stairs with both hands free was a boon. No long skirts to hold up or trip over!

Mrs. Stanton sighed and bent to her letter. Even the short dress was not going to free her to go to Rochester in less than three weeks. Well, she could still write, even if she couldn't travel.

"I will gladly do all in my power to help you," she continued. "Come and stay with me and I will write the best lecture I can for you. I have no doubt a little practice will make you an admirable speaker. Dress loosely, take a great deal of exercise, be particular about your diet and sleep enough. The body has great influence upon the mind. In your meetings, if attacked, be cool and good-natured . . . .

"As for my own address," she went on, "if I am to be president it ought perhaps to be sent out with the stamp of the convention, but as anything from my pen is necessarily radical no one may wish to share with me the odium[6] of what I may choose to say. If so, I am ready to stand alone."

Mrs. Stanton thought about the times she had had to be "cool and good-natured" when she was raging inside. Like the World Anti-slavery Convention which she and Henry had attended as newlyweds.

"I have been rereading the report of the London convention of 1840," she wrote. "How thoroughly humiliating it was to us! How I could have sat there quietly and listened to all that was said and done, I do not now understand. It is amazing that man can be so utterly unconscious of his brutality to women. . . . Men and angels give me patience! I am at the boiling point! If I do not find some day the use of my tongue on this

---

[6] disgrace

question, I shall die of an intellectual repression, a woman's rights convulsion! Oh, Susan! Susan! Susan!" she scribbled, "You must manage to spend a week with me before the Rochester convention, for I am afraid that I cannot attend it. I have so much care with all these boys on my hands. But I will write a letter. How much I do long to be free from housekeeping and children, so as to have some time to read, and think, and write."

Mrs. Stanton paused. She was expecting another baby, her fifth, in a few months. The freedom to "read, and think, and write" would not be coming soon, she thought with a sigh. "But it may be well for me to understand all the trials of woman's lot," she concluded, "that I may more eloquently proclaim them when the time comes. Good night."

Mrs. Stanton made it to the Rochester convention after all. She was elected president, and Susan, secretary. Although the purpose of their society was to promote temperance, Mrs. Stanton used her speech to talk about women's rights. She had some pretty strong opinions about divorce. She thought that women who were married to drunkards should be able to divorce them, and she proposed that drunkenness be made a legal reason for divorce. "Let no woman remain in the relation of wife with the confirmed drunkard," she declared. "Let no drunkard be the father of her children."

Mrs. Stanton had been quite right about her pen being too radical for most people. The newspapers attacked her and, at the next statewide meeting, a year later, Mrs. Stanton ran for reelection and lost. She resigned and so did Susan.

"You ask me if I am not plunged in grief at my defeat at the recent convention for the presidency of our society," Mrs. Stanton wrote to Susan afterward. "Not at all. I am only too happy in the relief I feel from this additional care. I accomplished at Rochester all I desired by having the divorce question brought up. . . . Now, Susan, I do beg of you to let the past be past, and to waste no powder on the Woman's State Temperance Society. We have other and bigger fish to fry."

* * *

How right Mrs. Stanton was! Not six months after that letter was written, she was preparing for one of the most important events of her life.

It was Susan's doing, really. Susan had come

up with a novel idea: to petition the New York State Legislature for equal rights. She had thought of it when she was trying to organize the temperance society. While touring the state, she had found that the local temperance groups had all disbanded because the women didn't have the money to keep them going. Most of the women were married, and their husbands owned the money. Even if a woman went out and earned money, by law it belonged to her husband.

"I never before took in so fully the grand idea of pecuniary[7] independence," Susan wrote in her diary. "Woman must have a purse[8] of her own, and how can this be, so long as the law denies to the wife all right to both the individual and joint earnings? There is no true freedom for woman without the possession of equal property rights, and these can be obtained only through legislation. If this be so the sooner the demand is made the sooner it will be granted. It must be done by petition, this too at the very next session of the legislature."

The plan was for Susan and other like-minded

---

[7] financial
[8] money

women to go door to door all over the state with petitions, getting signatures. The petitions would ask for new laws granting equal property rights and voting rights. Then, when the legislature met in Albany in February 1854, the women would present their petitions. At the same time, they would hold a state-wide women's rights convention. Finally, their most eloquent and powerful woman would speak before the legislature to persuade them to grant the petitions. And that woman, of course, would be Mrs. Stanton.

Mrs. Stanton herself was of two minds about Susan's plan. On the one hand, she thought it was extraordinary. The plan was big and it was bold. It would take tons of organization—halls to rent, ushers to hire, programs and speeches to be printed, dozens and dozens of letters to be written, the petitions—ugh! Mrs. Stanton shuddered at the thought. But Susan was good at that sort of thing.

On the other hand, Mrs. Stanton was still nursing her fifth child and she was weary. She had told Susan that she didn't want to be bothered with anything—not a single speech or letter. But here she was anyway, demanding not only Mrs. Stanton's thoughts, but her presence, too.

Well, if Susan was willing to take on the New York State Legislature, Mrs. Stanton could do no less. The Lord only knew where she'd find the time, but she would.

To tell the truth, Mrs. Stanton couldn't resist the idea of being the first woman ever to speak in the state capitol. She relished the thought of telling those men exactly what she thought of them. Well, maybe not *exactly* what she thought—it wouldn't be polite. But her blood was up. She'd write the best speech of her life.

It was a struggle, though. One night in December, an exhausted Mrs. Stanton sat down at her writing table. "Dear Susan," she wrote, "Can you get any acute lawyer—perhaps Judge Hay[9] is the man—sufficiently interested in our movement to look up just eight laws concerning us—the very worst in all the code? I can generalize and philosophize easily enough of myself; but the details of the particular laws I need, I have not time to look up. . . ."

Mrs. Stanton was pessimistic about the speech. She warned Susan to "prepare yourself to be disappointed in its merits, for I seldom have

[9] a friend and supporter of women's rights

one hour undisturbed in which to sit down and write."

Six weeks later, things were still hectic. "Yesterday one of the boys shot an arrow into my baby's eye," Mrs. Stanton reported. "The eye is safe, but oh! my fright when I saw the blood come and the organ swell, and witnessed her suffering! . . . Then, today, my nurse has gone home with a felon[10] on her finger, so you see how I am bound here."

As for the speech, it "is not nearly finished," she wrote, "but if I sit up nights, it shall be done in time."

✤✤✤

February 14, 1854, was a very special day in the history of the New York State Legislature. For the first time, a woman was to have a hearing before it. To be sure, most of the members already had their minds made up on this "woman" question. Nothing could convince them that married women should have their own money, or that women should vote, or that women should have equal rights of any sort.

---

[10] infection

Still they sat back, crossed their legs, and got ready to listen, for wasn't this Mrs. Henry Stanton, the wife of one of their own legislators from some years back? There she was now, entering the senate chamber. Very ladylike she looked, all in black silk with a white lace collar and a diamond pin. Uncommonly dignified the way she held her head up. Didn't appear nervous at all.

Mrs. Stanton stepped to the podium and quiet fell over the room. Taking one long look around, she began with a flourish, in the grand nineteenth century manner. "The tyrant, Custom" she declared in a clear, ringing voice, "has been summoned before the bar of Common Sense."

Now what did that mean? Did her audience understand her? They did, all right. They knew that by Custom, she meant all the traditions that put men over women, rich over poor, white over black, somebody over somebody else.

These traditions, she was saying, were like a monster. They had ruled far too many people's lives for far too long. "All nations, ranks, and classes" have struck down this cruel ruler, said she, ". . . and now that the monster is chained and caged, timid woman, on tiptoe, comes to look him in the face. . . ."

"Yes, gentlemen," Mrs. Stanton said with sudden directness, "in republican America, in the nineteenth century, we, the daughters of the revolutionary heroes of '76, demand at your hands a redress of our grievances—a revision of your State Constitution—a new code of laws. Permit us then, as briefly as possible, to call your attention to the legal disabilities under which we labor. . . ."

It was a brilliant speech. Within days, a copy of it appeared on the desk of every lawmaker—Susan's handiwork. She also had 20,000 copies printed up to be sold. For the next two weeks, the legislature, the newspapers, the convention, and the citizens of Albany were caught up in a whirlwind of women's rights.

It didn't take the legislature long to come to a decision. It voted to deny the petitions. Somehow, though, neither Susan nor Mrs. Stanton was really crushed by the defeat. They took the long view of things. Yes, they may have been beaten this time. They may have lost the battle, but the war was just beginning.

8

Susan Shocks the Teachers

It was hot in the hall and the air was stuffy. A man was giving a speech. Five hundred people fidgeted, fanned themselves, and doodled on their programs. The voice droned on.

Susan shifted impatiently in her seat and crossed and uncrossed her ankles. She sighed loudly. Was this man planning to talk them to death? He had been talking forever and had not said a thing. Oh thank heaven! He was sitting down at last. Now the president of the convention, Professor Davies from West Point, was recognizing someone else. That someone else got up, and began to drone on.

Susan was really at the end of her patience.

This was a convention of teachers, after all. These were people who were supposed to be able to solve problems. But they had been debating the same question for hours, and not once had they even come close to the point.

The question they were discussing was why the profession of teacher was not as much respected as that of doctor, lawyer, or minister. It was no mystery to Susan why this was so. To her the only mystery was why none of these learned gentlemen could figure it out.

She glanced around. A lot of the women looked bored—and no wonder. They weren't allowed to join the discussion. They were only there to listen. Who wouldn't be bored?

Well, they were about to become un-bored, all of them. Susan's heart began to pound. She waited for the speaker to finish. The minute he did, she stood up.

"Mr. President," she said.

At the sound of a female voice, a hush fell over the room. The fanning and fidgeting stopped. Everyone craned their necks to see who it was.

On the platform, Professor Davies looked bewildered for a moment. Then he drew himself up and puffed out his chest in its blue coat and gilt buttons.

"What will the lady have?" he asked commandingly.

"The lady would like to speak to the question under discussion," replied Susan.

What? Eyebrows flew up and mouths flew open. A woman? Address the convention? Everyone began talking at once. Over the commotion, Professor Davies thundered, "What is the pleasure of the convention?"

The clamor rose as scores of men shouted out at once. "She shall be heard!" cried one voice, louder than the rest. Another seconded the motion. Then for a full half-hour the men debated whether she *would* be heard.

Susan stayed on her feet as the argument swirled around her like a storm. Her knees were shaking so badly she was afraid to sit—she might not be able to get up again. She hadn't been this nervous since her first year of teaching. She took a deep breath to calm herself. She was not a schoolgirl anymore! She was a grown woman and she knew what she wanted to say. And if they'd give her half a chance, she'd say it.

At last a vote was taken—among the men only, of course. By a narrow margin, they voted to let Susan speak. She took another deep breath and began.

"It seems to me," she said, "that you fail to comprehend the cause of the disrespect of which you complain." She sounded as if she was scolding a class of children for being slow. "Do you not see that so long as society says woman has not brains enough to be a doctor, lawyer or minister, but has plenty to be a teacher, every man of you who condescends[11] to teach, tacitly[12] admits . . . that he has no more brains than a woman?"

Susan sat down. The hall was so silent, a pin could have been heard falling to the floor. Even Professor Davies was at a loss for words.

Suddenly three men broke the spell. They left their seats together and walked determinedly to where Susan sat. The whole room held its breath and watched, waiting to see what they would do to her. Then a loud chorus of indignant voices burst out all over the hall—the men were shaking her hand! They were *congratulating* her! Poor Professor Davies did the only thing left to do. He banged his gavel and adjourned for the day.

The next morning Susan was up early, drinking her coffee and reading about herself in the

---

[11] lowers himself
[12] silently

paper. Her disruption of the New York State Teachers Convention of 1853 had made headlines. One report pleased her particularly. The *Rochester Democrat* said that "whatever the school-masters might think of Miss Anthony, it was evident that she hit the nail on the head."

Good! That was exactly what she meant to do. She had come to this convention because it had put out a state-wide call for teachers. It hadn't said anything about *male* teachers. Well, she was a teacher—or had been. She believed she had every right to participate, so she did.

Still, no one likes being ridiculed. Especially not a sensitive soul like Susan. She couldn't help hearing the snide remarks that followed her as she left the hall. "Who can that creature be?" from one woman. "I was actually ashamed of my sex," from another. "She must be a dreadful woman to get up that way and speak in public," said a third, and so on.

Susan bore it without flinching. It only made her more determined. She decided that what the teachers of the state needed was a good strong dose of women's rights. Why not attend the New York State Teachers Convention every year, and shake them up? That's what she did.

She agitated for women's right to participate in debates, deliver essays, vote, and hold office— all the things the male teachers did. She argued that female teachers should make the same salaries as male teachers. And that girls and boys should receive the same education. Finally, after three years of this, the school-masters gave Susan a chance. They asked her to prepare a report on coeducation and deliver it at the 1856 convention.

Susan flew into a panic. Writing was her downfall. She was convinced that she had no talent for it. By the beginning of June, she had thought about her report and had even figured out how it should be organized. But she still hadn't started writing it. Instead, she wrote a long, desperate letter to Mrs. Stanton.

"And, Mrs. Stanton, not a *word written* on that Address for the Teacher's Convention . . . the Mercy only knows when I can get a moment; and what is *worse,* as the *Lord knows full well,* if I get *all the time* the *world has,* I *can't get up* a *decent document.* So, for the love of me and for the saving of the *reputation* of *womanhood,* I beg you, with one baby on your knee and another at your feet, and four boys whistling, buzzing, hallooing *Ma, Ma,* set yourself about the work. It is of but small moment[13] *who writes* the Address, but of *vast moment* that it be *well done.* . . . Now will *you load my gun,* leaving me only to pull the trigger and let fly the powder and ball?

"Don't delay one mail to tell me what you *will do,* for I *must not* and *will not* allow these *schoolmasters* to say—See, these *women can't* or *won't* do anything when we do give them a chance. . . . Do get all on fire and be as *cross* as you please. You remember, Mr. Stanton told how cross you always get over a speech. Good Bye."

Mrs. Stanton had never been busier. She now had six children, the youngest just six months old. But how could she say no to Susan? She couldn't.

"Your servant is not dead but liveth," Mrs. Stanton wrote back. "Imagine me, day in and day out, watching, bathing, dressing, nursing, and promenading the precious contents of a little crib in the corner of the room. I pace up and down these two chambers of mine like a caged lioness. . . . Is your speech to be exclusively on the point of educating the sexes together, or as to the best manner of educating women? I will do what I can to help you. . . ."

---

[13] importance

She was as good as her word. Susan showed up at the Stantons' door, suitcase in hand, and they set to work in the parlor, at a big round table littered with papers and books opened every which way. Susan had the facts at her command, and Mrs. Stanton had the words. For hours on end they talked, argued, laughed, and wrote. There were countless interruptions, but they kept at it. Mrs. Stanton did most of the writing, while Susan made changes and corrections as they went along.

The speech, called "Educating the Sexes Together," was finished in time for Susan to deliver it in August. In it, she exploded the common idea that female brains were smaller and therefore weaker than male brains. She argued that in mind, soul, and thought, there was no difference between men and women. Thus the same education was necessary for both sexes. And in that case, why educate them separately?

It was as if Susan had thrown a bomb into the midst of the convention. When she left the podium and returned to her seat on the platform, the president of the convention turned to her. "As much as I am compelled to admire . . . your address and its delivery," he said, "I would rather follow a

daughter of mine to her grave, than to have her deliver such an address before such an assembly."

But another official, overhearing the remark, disagreed. "I should be proud, Madam," said he, "if I had a daughter capable of making such an eloquent and finished argument, before this or any assembly of men and women. I congratulate you on your triumphant success."

Whether the report was a triumph or not depended on your point of view. Susan and Mrs. Stanton thought it was. The next year Susan dropped another bombshell. She proposed a resolution condemning the exclusion of black children from the public schools. And she proposed a resolution that said "it is the duty of all our schools, colleges and universities to open their doors to woman and to give her equal and identical educational advantages side by side with her brother man."

Though the resolutions were defeated, the papers had much to say about Susan. "Miss Anthony vindicated her resolutions," said the *Binghamton Daily Republican*, "with great eloquence, spirit, and dignity, and showed herself a match, at least, in debate, for any member of the Convention. She was *equal* if not *identical*."

Mrs. Stanton, at home as always, was pleased as punch. "Dear Susan," she wrote, "I did indeed see by the papers that you had once more stirred . . . the education convention. The *Times* was really quite complimentary. Henry brought me every item he could see about you. 'Well,' he would say, 'another notice about Susan. You stir up Susan, and she stirs the world.'"

True enough. And didn't Susan also stir up Mrs. Stanton, bringing her news from the front lines, where she longed to be but couldn't? Together, it was said, they were like "two sticks of a drum, keeping up . . . 'the rub-a-dub of agitation.'"

"I will do anything to help you on," Mrs. Stanton promised. "You must come here for a week or two and we will accomplish wonders. You and I have a prospect of a good long life. We shall not be in our prime before fifty, and after that we shall be good for twenty years at least. . . ."

9

Through the Years

The work that Susan and Mrs. Stanton did together in the 1850s was just the beginning. Each passing year found them working just as hard as ever for women's rights. There were setbacks, and they made mistakes, but they never, ever gave up.

When the Civil War came in 1861, women's rights faded from most people's minds—even from the minds of many women's rights leaders. The war was all-consuming. Susan and Mrs. Stanton founded the Women's Loyal League, a group that raised money for the Union side. Mrs. Stanton thought that if women put their effort into winning the war and freeing the slaves, then later on, when the war ended, abolitionists and Union supporters would help women win the vote.

She was wrong, though. When the war ended, the Fifteenth Amendment to the Constitution was ratified. It defined a citizen as a male, and guaranteed the right to vote and hold office to all males, regardless of race. So black men won the right to vote, finally, but women of all races still couldn't vote.

The worst of it was, in Susan and Mrs. Stanton's eyes, that in the fight over the amendment, the abolitionists turned their backs on women. Frederick Douglass, William Lloyd Garrison, Wendell Phillips—all their staunchest allies over the years—refused to support an amendment that would include race *and* sex. Even some prominent women refused to support such an amendment. They were afraid they couldn't win. They thought it was more important for black men to have their rights—a sure thing—than to try to win equal rights for everyone and lose.

This was a bitter lesson for the two women. They realized that they couldn't rely on men to help them in their fight. They could rely only on themselves. In 1868, they founded the National Woman Suffrage Association. This was an organization for women only, dedicated to winning the right to vote.

Though Mrs. Stanton was president for many years, seemingly in charge, it was Susan who built the organization. It was Susan who, year in and year out, organized and attended conventions, circulated petitions, and traveled endlessly from town to town. She spoke in churches, halls, barns, parlors, even saloons, to recruit members. Yes, Susan. The frightened, homesick girl had turned into a woman who never stayed in one place long. The little diaries she kept all her life showed new towns, different hotels, and strange audiences nearly every day for weeks and months on end.

Mrs. Stanton didn't stay at home all her life, either. Beginning in the late 1860s, when her seven children were all nearly grown, she too began to travel. In 1867, she and Susan toured Kansas, speaking in favor of suffrage for women and blacks. Three years later they went to California to campaign for woman suffrage. Throughout the 1870s, Mrs. Stanton traveled the country for eight months a year as a paid lecturer, spending only Christmas and summers at home. Her subject was always women's rights.

Susan and Mrs. Stanton managed to make news in the 1870s. For a while they published a controversial women's rights newspaper called *Revolution*. Susan handled the business end, while Mrs. Stanton wrote and edited. In 1872, Susan was arrested for voting in a presidential election. In 1878, Mrs. Stanton persuaded Senator Aaron A. Sargent of California to introduce a federal amendment into Congress granting women suffrage.

By 1880, when she was 65, Mrs. Stanton had grown tired of "wandering on the western prairies." She decided to stay home and devote herself to writing. By this time the Stantons had left Seneca Falls and lived in Tenafly, New Jersey. Susan came to stay with her and they began writing *The History of Woman Suffrage*. What started out as a pamphlet grew into one volume, then two. When it was finished, the history was six volumes long.

Mrs. Stanton, doing the writing, enjoyed herself thoroughly. Susan hated it. "I am just sick to death of the whole of it," she wrote. "I had rather wash or whitewash or any possible hard work than sit here and go digging into the dusty records of the past—that is rather *make* history than *write* it."

As Susan and Mrs. Stanton entered old age, they found themselves going in different directions. Though they were still friends—nothing could change that—they had different ideas about what women should be doing to gain their rights. Susan thrived on organizing and managing. By the late 1880s, she had built an organization of thousands of women dedicated to winning the vote. Mostly of a younger generation, they were devoted to her. She was "Aunt Susan" and they were her "girls."

Susan had come to see suffrage as the answer to all of women's problems and she would not be diverted from this theme. What she had to do, she realized, was make suffrage respectable. She had to make it something that ordinary women and men could accept. She was successful. For example, when the first suffrage petition was circulated in 1854, it got 4,000 signatures. In 1894, forty years later, the same petition got 500,000 signatures!

But becoming respectable also meant avoiding controversy, which brought Susan into direct conflict with her old friend. For Mrs. Stanton had never stopped being controversial. In her old age, this woman who had first demanded the vote began to think that voting wasn't the answer. Or at least, voting wasn't the only answer. She grew irritated with Susan, who thought it was. "Miss Anthony has one idea," Mrs. Stanton wrote tartly in 1896, "and she has no patience with anyone who has two."

The target of Mrs. Stanton's anger—and her pen—became religion. She firmly believed that the church was keeping women in bondage. She criticized Christianity and Judaism because, she said, they taught that woman is inferior to man. She attacked ministers and rabbis and she criticized the Bible. She even went so far as to publish *The Woman's Bible*, which contained passages from the Bible along with her own scathing commentaries. What most people held sacred, Mrs. Stanton seemed to trample underfoot in the name of women's rights.

So while Susan worked to make suffrage respectable, Mrs. Stanton sent out shock waves. "I get more and more radical as I grow older," wrote Mrs. Stanton in her diary, "while she seems to get more conservative." It was true, and it pulled them apart. But it didn't destroy them.

In June of 1902, Susan visited Mrs. Stanton at home for the last time. Susan, at 82, wore spectacles all the time. Her white hair was pulled back into the same old-fashioned bun she had worn for decades. Her lean features gave her a stern, joyless air. Indeed, she could be stern on occasion. But joyless—never.

Mrs. Stanton was, as always, impeccably dressed. Her curls were a beautiful snowy white, lovely against the black silk she always wore. But her health was failing, anyone could see it. She had grown immensely fat in her old age. She needed two canes just to stand. And she was completely blind.

"It seems good to be here," Susan had written in her diary, "though Mrs. Stanton does not feel quite as she used to. We have grown a little apart since not so closely associated as of old. She thinks the Church is now the enemy to fight and feels worried that I stay back with the children[14] as she says—instead of going ahead with her."

When the time came to leave, all the old feel-

<hr />

[14] the younger members of the suffrage movement

ings welled up in Susan. Putting her arms around Mrs. Stanton, she started to cry.

"Shall I see you again?" she asked.

"Oh yes," Mrs. Stanton replied, dry-eyed. "If not here, then in the hereafter, if there is one, and if there isn't we shall never know it."

Susan said good-bye then, and promised to come back in November for Mrs. Stanton's 87th birthday.

Epilogue

Susan was sitting in near total darkness when her sister Mary knocked softly at her door. Dusk came so early on those late fall days, and Susan hadn't lit the lamp. The telegram still lay in her lap. As she looked outside her window, her eyes came to rest on a distant point of pale sky above the black treetops.

Suddenly Susan blinked, startled. Mary stood there in the gloom. She had come to ask if Susan would walk downstairs and meet with the reporters. They had been swarming around the house all afternoon. Susan hadn't even noticed them.

The sisters descended to the parlor together,

Susan leaning on Mary's arm. The room was full of reporters, eager to know what the famous Susan B. Anthony was feeling at the death of her equally famous friend. Ida Harper and the secretary were there, too. They started making arrangements for Susan to go to New York the next day for the funeral.

All the while Susan sat like a rock. She was silent except when she tried to answer questions. Then she would hesitate painfully. Her gnarled hands seemed to tremble with the effort. "I cannot express myself at all as I feel," she said at last. "I am too crushed to speak. If I had died first she would have found beautiful phrases to describe our friendship, but I cannot put it into words."

Susan left for New York City the next day to attend Mrs. Stanton's funeral. "Well, it is an awful hush," she wrote to Ida Harper from New York, "it seems impossible—that the voice is hushed that I have longed to hear for fifty years. . . . It is all at sea—but the Laws of Nature are still going on—with no shadow or turning—what a wonder it is—it goes right on and on—no matter who lives or who dies."

Life went on for Susan for four more years. In spite of a weak heart, she continued to travel and make speeches for suffrage, as she had done all her life. The last time she spoke publicly was at a big celebration held for her 86th birthday in Washington, D.C. She was very ill by then.

Sitting on the platform, Susan listened to speeches praising her and messages of congratulation from the Congress and President Roosevelt. Finally it was her turn to speak. She stood weakly, holding onto the shoulder of one of the younger women. Gazing out over the sea of adoring faces, she struggled to find words. Thanking them, she tried to say that she didn't deserve all the honor. "There have been others also," she said, "just as true and devoted to the cause—I wish I could name every one—but with such women consecrating[15] their lives—failure is impossible."

Susan B. Anthony died a month later. In 1920, fourteen years after her death, the Nineteenth Amendment to the United States Constitution was ratified. It guarantees that the right to vote or hold office shall not be denied to any citizen on account of sex.

---

[15] dedicating

Afterword

All of the conversations and speeches that appeared in quotation marks in the preceding pages are from documented sources. The letters, diaries, reminiscences, and other works of Susan B. Anthony and Elizabeth Cady Stanton provided the foundation of *They Shall Be Heard*. Also helpful were biographies of the two women by Katharine Anthony, Kathleen Barry, Ellen Carol DuBois, Elisabeth Griffith, Ida Harper, Alma Lutz, and Cecil Roseberry.

Notes

Pages 17-18 Among the Americans who attended the World Anti-Slavery Convention was William Lloyd Garrison, one of the most famous abolitionists of his time. Garrison, who had struggled for equal rights for women in the American Anti-Slavery Society, believed that the women delegates had every right to participate in the convention. In protest of the vote to bar women, Garrison sat with them in the area set aside for women and observers.

Page 19 Lucretia Coffin Mott was a member of the Religious Society of Friends, more commonly known as Quakers. The Society arose in England in the mid-

17th century, and had always given women equality in worship. In fact, there were Quaker women preachers in Massachusetts and Maryland as early as 1656.

At a Friends service, called a "meeting," Quakers gather together, often silently, to worship and await God's word. A Quaker who has reached a new insight or understanding may arise and speak to the congregation. It does not matter whether the speaker is male or female. The people at the meeting then weigh this "testimony" in light of their own spiritual experience.

Pages 23–24 While the Declaration of Sentiments was passed in its entirety, Mrs. Stanton's resolution demanding the right to vote was the only resolution that did not pass unanimously. In fact, it was the subject of a great deal of debate, and just barely passed. It took a speech by Frederick Douglass, the great orator and ex-slave, to persuade a majority of those present to vote in favor of the resolution. Douglass said that he would not dare claim a right for himself that he would not concede to women.

Page 28 Daniel and Lucy Anthony eventually had seven children. At this time, however, only Guelma, Susan, and Hannah had been born. Had the Anthonys taken in eleven mill hands after all the children had been born, they would have been cooking three meals each day for twenty people.

Page 31 It is not clear from Susan's reminiscences whether the incident concerning Daniel Anthony's refusal to pay taxes occurred during a time of peace or war, or even whether there was more than one incident of this sort. If the incident did occur during wartime, the war was most probably the Mexican War, which lasted from 1846 to 1848.

Page 49 Although the bloomer outfit was popularized by Amelia Bloomer, it was actually created by Mrs. Stanton's cousin, Elizabeth Smith Miller, who wore it when she visited Mrs. Stanton in Seneca Falls in 1851. Mrs. Stanton adopted the dress immediately. She wore the "short dress," as women's rights leaders called it, for two years. Mrs. Stanton stopped wearing it in public because of the ridicule it caused. She feared that controversy over the dress would distract people from more important issues such as the struggle for women's right to vote.

It took Mrs. Stanton six months, until December of 1852, to persuade Susan to wear the short dress. But then Susan was one of the last to stop wearing it. Susan suffered greatly from the attention it drew, but felt that to give up the short dress would be a defeat. In the winter of 1854, Mrs. Stanton wrote to her: "I hope, Susan, you have let down a dress and petticoat. The cup of ridicule is greater than you can bear. It is not wise, Susan, to use up so much energy in that way." Finally, Susan, too, went back to the traditional long dress. The reason, she said, was that when she wore the short dress, she "never could get rid of thinking of herself, and the important thing is to forget self. The attention of my audience was fixed upon my clothes instead of my words."

Kate Connell lives in New York where she works as a writer and editor. Ms. Connell is also the author of *Tales from the Underground Railroad* and *These Lands Are Ours*.